THE LIFE OF BUDDHA
AND
ITS LESSONS

THE LIFE OF BUDDHA AND ITS LESSONS

BY
H.S. OLCOTT

ISBN: 978-93-5128-671-4(HB)

First Published in 1906
Indian Reprint in 2017

Published by

Kalpaz Publications
C-30, Satyawati Nagar,
Delhi – 110052
E-mail: kalpaz@hotmail.com
Website: kalpazpublications.com
Ph.: +91-9212142040

The thoughtful student, in scanning the religious history of the race has one fact continually forced upon his notice, *viz.*, that there is an invariable tendency to deify whomsoever shows himself superior to the weakness of our common humanity. Look where we will, we find the saint like man exalted into a divine personage and worshiped for a god. Though perhaps misunderstood, reviled and even persecuted while living, the apotheosis is almost sure to come after death: and the victim of yesterday's mob, raised to the stage of an Intercessor in Heaven, is besought with prayer and tears, and placatory penances to mediate with God for the pardon of human sin. This is a mean and vile trait of human nature, the proof of ignorance, selfishness, brutal cowardice, and a superstitious materialism. It shows the base instinct to put down and destroy whatever or whoever makes men feel their own imperfections; with the alternative of ignoring and denying these very imperfections by turning into gods men who have merely spiritualized their natures, so that it may be supposed that they were heavenly incarnations and not mortal like other men.

This process of *enhemerisation*, as it is called, or the making of men into gods and gods into men, sometimes, though more rarely, begins during the life of the hero, but usually after death. The true history of his life is gradually amplified and decorated with fanciful incidents, to fit it to the new character which has been posthumously given him. Omens and portents are now made to attend his earthly avatâra: his precocity is described as superhuman: as a babe or lisping child he silences the wisest logicians by his divine knowledge: miracles he produces as other boys do soap-bubbles: the terrible energies of nature are his playthings: the gods, angels, and demons are his habitual attendants: the sun, moon, and all the starry host wheel around his cradle in joyful measures, and the earth thrills with joy at having borne such a prodigy: and at his last hour of mortal life the whole universe shakes with conflicting emotions.

Why need I use the few moments at my disposal to marshal before you the various personages of whom these fables have been written? Let it suffice to recall the interesting fact to your notice, and invite you to compare the respective biographies of the Brâhmanical Krshna, the Persian Zoroaster, the Egyptian Hermes, the Indian Gautama, and the canonical, especially the apocryphal, Jesus. Taking Krshna or Zoroaster, as you please, as the most ancient, and coming down the chronological line of descent, you will find them made after the same pattern. The real personage is all covered up and concealed under the embroidered veils of the romancer and the enthusiastic historiographer. What is surprising to me is that this tendency to exaggeration and hyperbole is not more commonly allowed for by those who in our days attempt to discuss and compare religions. We are constantly and painfully reminded that the prejudice of inimical critics, on the one hand, and the furious bigotry of devotees, on the other, blind men to fact and probability, and lead to gross injustice. Let me take as an example the mythical biographies of Jesus. At the time when the Council of Nicea was convened for settling the quarrels of certain bishops and for the purpose of examining into the canonicity of the hundred more or less apocryphal gospels, that were being read in the Christian churches as inspired writings, the history of the life of Christ has reached the height of absurd myth. We may see some specimens in the extant books of the apocryphal New Testament, but most of them are now lost. What have been retained in the present canon may doubtless be regarded as the least objectionable. And yet, we must not hastily adopt even this conclusion, for you know that Sabina, Bishop of Heracha, himself speaking of the Council of Nicea affirms that "except Constantine and Sabinus, Bishop of Pamphilus, these bishops were a set of illiterate, simple creatures, that understood nothing;" which is as though he had said they were a pack of fools. And Pappus, in his *Synodicon* to that Council of Nicea, lets us into the secret that the canon was not decided by a careful comparison of several gospels before them, but by a *lottery*. Having, he tells us, "promiscuously put all the 'books that were referred to the Council for determination under a Communion table in a church, they (the bishops) besought the Lord that the inspired writings might get up on the table, while the spurious writings remained underneath, and *it happened accordingly*'. But letting all this pass and looking only to what is contained in the present canon, we see the same tendency to compel all nature to attest the divinity of the writer's hero. At the nativity a star leaves its orbit and leads the Persian astrologers to the divine and angels come and converse with shepherds, and a whole train of like celestial phenomena occurs at various stages of his earthly career, which closes amid earthquakes, a pall of darkness over the whole scene, a supernatural war of the elements, the opening of graves and walking about of their tenants and other appalling wonders. Now, if the candid Buddhist concedes that the real history of Gautama is embellished by like absurd exaggerations, and if we can find their duplicates in the biographies of Zoroaster, Shankarâchâya and the other real personages of antiquity, have we not the right to conclude that the true history of the Founder of Christianity, if at this late date it were possible to write it, would be very different from the narratives that pass current? We must not forget that Jerusalem was at that time a Roman dependency, just as Ceylon is now a British, and that the silence of contemporary Roman historians about any such violent disturbances of the equilibrium of nature is deeply significant.

I have cited this example for the sole and simple purpose of bringing home to the non-Buddhistic portion of my present audience the conviction that, in considering the life of Sâkya Muni and the lessons it teaches, they must not make his followers of today responsible for any extravagant exuberances of past' biographers. The doctrine of Buddha and its effects are to be judged quite apart from the man, just as the doctrine ascribed to Jesus and its effects are to be considered quite irrespectively from his personal history.

And— as I hope I have shown the actual doings and sayings of every founder of a faith or a school of philosophy, must be sought for under a heap of tinsel and rubbish contributed by successive generations of followers.

Approaching the question of the hour in this spirit of precaution, what do we find are the probabilities respecting the life of Sâkya Muni? Who was he? When did he live? How did he live? What did he teach? A most careful comparison of authorities and analysis of evidence establishes, I think, the following data:

1. He was the son of a King

2. He lived between six and seven centuries before Christ

3. He resigned his royal state and went to live in the jungle, and among the lowest and most unhappy classes, so as to learn the secret of human pain and misery by personal experience: tested every known austerity of the Hindû ascetics and excelled them all in his power of endurance: sounded every depth of woe in search of the means to alleviate it: and at last came out victorious, and showed the world the way to salvation.

4. What he taught may be summed up in a few words, as the perfume of many roses may be distilled into a few drops of *attar*: Everything in the world of matter is unreal; the only reality is the world of Spirit.

Emancipate yourselves from the tyranny of the former; strive to attain the latter. The Rev. Samuel Beal, in his *Catena of Buddhist Scriptures from the Chinese* puts it differently. "The idea underlying the Buddhist religious system is," he says, "simply this 'all is vanity'. Earth is a show, and Heaven is a vain reward." Primitive Buddhism was engrossed , absorbed by one thought, the vanity of finite existence, the priceless value of the one condition of Eternal Rest.

If I have the temerity to prefer my own definition of the spirit of Buddha's doctrine it is because I think that all the misconceptions of it have arisen from a failure to understand his idea of what is real and what is unreal, what worth longing and striving for and what not. From this misconception have come all the unfounded charges that Buddhism is an 'atheistical,' that is to say, a grossly materialistic, a nihilistic, a negative, a vice-breeding religion. Buddhism denies the existence of a personal God — true; therefore — well, therefore, and notwithstanding all this, its teaching is neither what may be called properly atheistical, nihilistic, negative nor provocative of vice. I will try to make my meaning clear, and the advancement of modern scientific research helps in this direction. Science divides the universe for us into two elements — matter and force; accounting for their phenomena by their combinations, and making both eternal and obedient to eternal and immutable law. The speculations of men of science have carried them to the outermost verge of the physical universe. Behind them lie not only a thousand brilliant triumphs by which a part of Nature's secrets have been wrung from her, but also more thousands of failures to fathom her deep mysteries. They have proved thought material, since it is the evolution of the gray tissue of the brain, and a recent German experimentalist, Professor Dr Jäger, claims to have proved that man's soul is "a volatile odoriferous principle, capable of solution in glycerine". Psychogen is the name he gives to it, and his experiments show that it is present not merely in the body as a whole, but in every individual cell, in the ovum, and even in the ultimate elements of protoplasm. I need hardly say to so intelligent an audience as this that these highly interesting experiments of Dr Jäger are corroborated by many facts, both physiological and psychological that have been always noticed among all nations; facts which are woven into popular proverbs, legends, folk-lore fables, mythologies and theologies, the world over. Now, if thought is matter and soul is matter, then Buddha in recognizing the impermanence of sensual enjoyment or experience of any kind, and the instability of every material form, the human soul included, uttered a profound and scientific truth. And since the very idea of gratification or suffering is inseparable from that of material being — absolute SPIRIT alone being regarded by common consent as perfect, changeless and Eternal — therefore, in teaching the doctrine, that conquest of the material self, with all its lusts, desires, loves, hopes, ambitions and hates, frees one from pain, and leads to Nirvâna, the state of Perfect Rest, he preached the rest of an untinged, untainted existence in the Spirit. Though the soul be composed of the finest conceivable substance, yet if substance at all — as Dr Jäger seems able to prove, and ages of human intercourse with the weird phantoms of the shadow world imply — it must in time perish. What remains is that changeless part of man, which most philosophers call Spirit, and Nirvâna is its necessary condition of existence. The only dispute between Buddhist authorities is whether this Nirvânic existence is attended with individual consciousness, or whether the individual is merged in the whole, as the extinguished flame is lost in the air. But there are those who say that the flame has not been annihiliated by the blowing out. It has only passed out of the visible world of matter into the invisible world of Spirit, where it still exists and will ever exist, as a bright reality. Such thinkers can understand Buddha's doctrine and, while agreeing with him that soul is not immortal, would spurn the charge of materialistic nihilism if brought against either that sublime teacher or themselves.

The history of Sâkya Muni's life is the strongest bulwark of his religion. As long as the human heart is capable of being touched by tales of heroic self-sacrifice, accompanied by purity and celestial benevolence of motive, it will cherish his memory. Why should I go into the particulars of that noble life?

You will remember that he was the son of the king of Kapilavastu — a mighty sovereign whose opulence enabled him to give the heir of the house every luxury that a voluptuous imagination could desire: and that the future Buddha was not allowed to even know, much less observe, the miseries of ordinary existence. How beautifully Edwin Arnold has painted for us in *The Light of Asia* the luxury and languor of that Indian Court, "where love was gaoler and delights its bars." We are told that:

> The king commanded that within those walls
> No mention should be made of age or death,
> Sorrow or pain, or sickness . . . . . .
> And every dawn the dying rose was plucked,
> The dead leaves hid, all evil sights removed;
> For said the king, "If he shall pass his youth
> Far from such things as move to wistfulness
> And brooding on the empty eggs of thought,
> The shadow of this fate, too vast for man,
> May fade, belike, and I shall see him grow
> To that great stature of fair sovereignty,
> When he shall rule all lands — if he *will rule* —
> The king of kings and glory of his time'

You know how vain were all the precautions taken by the father to prevent the fulfilment of the prophecy that his beloved son would be the coming Buddha. Though all suggestions of death were banished from the royal palace, though the city was bedecked in flowers and gay flags, and every painful object removed from sight when the young Prince Siddartha visited the city, yet the decrees of destiny were not to be baffled, the "voices of the spirits," the "wandering winds," and the devas whispered the truth of human sorrows into his listening ear, and when the appointed hour arrived, the Suddha Devas threw the spell of slumber over the household, steeped in profound lethargy the sentinels (as we are told was done by an angel to the gaoler's of Peter's prison). rolled back the triple gates of bronze, strewed the sweet moghra flowers thickly beneath his horse's feet to muffle every sound, and he was free, free? Yes — to resign every earthly comfort, every sensuous enjoyment, the sweets of royal power, the homage of a court, the delights of domestic life: gems, the glitter of gold: rich stuffs, rich food, soft beds: the songs of trained musicians, and of birds kept prisoners in gay cages, the murmur of perfumed waters plashing in marble basins, the delicious shade of trees in gardens where art had contrived to make nature even lovelier than herself. He leaps from his saddle when at a safe distance from the palace, flings the jeweled rein to his faithful groom, Channa, cuts off his flowing locks, gives his rich costume to a hunter in exchange for his own, plunges into the jungle, and is free:

To tread its paths with patient, stainless feet,
Making its dusty bed, its loneliest wastes
My dwelling, and its meanest things my mates;
Clad in no prouder garb than outcasts wear,
Fed with no meals save what the charitable
Give of their will, sheltered by no more pomp,
Than the dim cave lends or the jungle-bush.
This will I do because the woeful cry
Of life and all flesh living cometh up
Into my ears, and all my soul is full
Of pity for the sickness of this world:
Which I will heal, if healing may be found
By uttermost renouncing and strong strife.

Thus masterfully does Sir Edwin Arnold depict the sentiment which provoked this Great Renunciator. The testimony of thousands of millions who, during the last twenty-five centuries have professed the Buddhistic religion, proves that the secret of human misery was at least solved by this divine selfsacrifice, and the true path to Nirvâna opened.

The joy that he brought to the hearts of others, Buddha first tasted himself. He found that the pleasures of the eye, the ear, the taste, touch and smell are fleeting and deceptive: he who gives value to them brings only disappointment and bitter sorrow upon himself. The social differences between men he found were equally arbitrary and illusive; caste bred hatred and selfishness; riches strife, envy and malice. So in founding his faith he laid the bottom of its foundation-stones upon all this worldly dirt, and its dome in the clear serene of the world of Spirit. He who can mount to a clear conception of Nirvâna will find his thought far away above the common joys and sorrows of petty men. As to one who ascends to the top of Chimborazo or the Himâlayan crags, and sees men on the earth's surface crawling to and fro like ants, so equally small do bigots and sectarians appear to him. The mountain climber has under his feet the very clouds from whose sun-painted shapes the poet has figured to himself the golden streets and glittering domes of the matcrialistic Heaven of a personal God. Below him are all the various objects out of which the world's pantheons have been manufactured: around, above — Immensity. And so also, far down the ascending plane of thought that leads from the earth towards the Infinite, the philosophic Buddhist describes at different plateaux the heavens and hells, the gods and demons of the materialistic creed-builders.

What are the lessons to be derived from the life and teachings of this heroic prince of Kapilavastu? Lessons of gratitude and benevolence. Lessons of tolerance for the clashing opinions of men who live, move and have their being, think and aspire only in the material world. The lesson of a common tie of brotherhood among all men. Lessons of manly self-reliance, of equanimity in breasting whatsoever of good or ill may happen. Lessons of the meanness of the rewards, the pettiness of the misfortunes of a shifting world of illusions. Lessons of the necessity for avoiding every species of evil thought and word, and for doing, speaking and thinking everything that is good, and for the bringing of the mind into subjection so that these may be accomplished, without selfish motive or vanity. Lessons of selfpurification and communion by which the illusiveness of externals and the value of internals are understood.

Well might St. Hilaire burst into the panegyric that Buddha "is the prefect model of all the virtues he preaches . . . . his life has not a stain upon it". Well might the sober critic Max Müller pronounce his moral code 'one of the most perfect which the world has ever known". No wonder that in contemplating that gentle life Edwin Arnold should have found his personality "the highest, gentlest, holiest and most beneficent . . . . in the history of thought," and been moved to write his splendid verses. It is twenty-five hundred years since humanity put forth such a flower: who knows when it did before?

Gautama Buddha Sâkya Muni, has ennobled the whole human race. His fame is our common inheritance. His Law is the law of Justice providing for every good thought, word and deed its fair reward, for every evil one its proper punishment. His law is in harmony with the voices of nature, and the evident equilibrium of the universe. It yields nothing to importunities or threats, can be neither coaxed nor bribed by offerings to abate or alter one jot or title of its inexorable course. Am I told that Buddhist laymen display vanity in their worship and ostentation in their alms-giving: that they are fostering sects as bitterly as Hindûs. So much the worse for the laymen: there is the example of Buddha and his law. Am I told that Buddhist priests are ignorant, idle fosterers of superstitions grafted on their religion by foreign kings? So much the worse for the priests; the life of their Divine Master shames them and shows their unworthiness to wear his yellow robe or carry his beggar-bowl. There is the Law — immutable — menacing; it will find them out and punish.

And what shall we say to those of another caste of character — the humble-minded, charitable, tolerant, religiously aspiring hearts among the laity, and the unselfish, pure and learned of the priest who know the Precepts and keep them? The Law will find them out also; and when the book of each life is written up and the balance struck, every good thought or deed will be found entered in its proper place. Not one blessing that ever followed them from grateful lips throughout their earthly pilgrimage will be found to have been lost; but each will help to ease their way as they move from stage to stage of Being.